M000205580

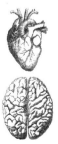

CRYBABY
Caitlyn Siehl

WORDS DANCE PUBLISHING
WordsDance.com

1st Edition
ISBN-13: 978-0692732243
ISBN-10: 0692732241

Cover photo by Jewel Beddia
Cover design & interior layout by Amanda Oaks

Type set in WC Mano Negra, New York & Bergamo.

Words Dance Publishing
WordsDance.com

heal loudly

CRYBABY
Caitlyn Siehl

CRYBABY

TASTING THE MOON

I am thinking about
the crescent scar on the
roof of his mouth that he
got when he fell with
a straw between his teeth

and how it felt to run my tongue
over it.

How it felt to taste the moon.

If love is anything tangible, it
is his mouth,

his mouth,

his holy goddamned mouth.

He says my name
and the whole sky is talking.

GOLDEN

We are wanted.

All bright-faced and
golden and heavy and
smooth.

So delicate it is almost barbaric,
almost violent.

We are unbearably,
intolerably
soft.

Nothing can touch us but everything
wants to.

Love would kill us in our sleep
just to get inside of us.

WINTER SHOES

Sideswept, windswept,
I want to keep your coat
in my closet forever.

Leave your boots in my doorway
until the salt on them makes rings
on the hardwood floor.

Unbreak my bedroom, quiet
the lamp in my throat.
Turn it off and stay until my blinds
aren't dusty.

My favorite dream I've ever had
is the one where you aren't wearing
shoes in the middle of Newark Airport.
I don't know where you were going
but your feet stopped me dead
in my tracks.

I fell to my knees and through the
floor and into some silence that
talked like you.
When I woke up, I was water.
My sheets, my face, my covers;
all water.

Play tic-tac-toe on my legs with
your one sharp nail while I read.
Walk through the front door
like it's Christmas and I'm not
making this up.

Come back to the island. My island.
Your absence is the best company
I've ever had but I think you
might be better.

MOST OF THE TIME

A hand on my thigh. That is
what I'm thinking about,
most of the time.

A hand slipping under my dress,
the other holding the steering wheel,
and me, upright in the passenger's
seat.

Fearless.
Always fearless in love, like
I've had practice.

Look, I know you're sick of
hearing about the skin of it all, but
I'm not done being shameless
with where I want to be touched.

A hand pressed lightly against
my neck. Lips grazing
the apple of my bottom lip.
Your name like a tongue
over the ridges of my teeth.
Your body like a downpour
with me dancing underneath it.

UNREMARKABLE

Mara tells me that he was
no one special.

Okay.
I believe her.

He was no one special.
Unremarkable, even.
A newspaper man with coffee
breath and ugly sneakers.

Mara tells me to let go.

But I waited for him, Mara.
I ate the scraps of his heart like
a starving dog under the dinner
table.

I slept at his feet
and then by the door
when he was too far
away.

I dreamt of coffee.
I brought the newspaper in
every morning.

He was no one special, but it
didn't matter, Mara,
because I kissed his stained teeth.
I brushed his unremarkable hair,
rested my head on his soft,
unremarkable stomach.

There was no hunger like my
hunger, Mara.
No man like my plain man.
No torch like my torch.

THE MASK

What did you sound like when
God, afraid to get his teeth dirty,
ate you with his stomach
like a starfish?

I think you were afraid. I think,
for all your talk of salvation,
you walked into that light
with rattlesnake knees,
buckling completely
when the light turned out to be
pitch black and growling.

I'm not saying that God
is a monster,
I'm saying that there wasn't
an open arm in sight when he came
to you,
that maybe
he lied a little bit
about all the glory,
the white soft cloud of it all.

That maybe
you had more love before
you took his.

QUIET DEATH

Mother, if you really want to know,
Yes.
I wanted to die for her.
I wanted to lay down
in the middle of the street
and die for her.

I play shadow puppets with her memory;
drink champagne until
I'm tender.

She is the grave
I don't know how
to talk about.
The one that I survived.
The one that I came crawling
out of, fingernails bent back.

The one that bagged my groceries
and didn't look at me
the right way,
the way I wanted her to.

Mother, her
absence was the most
beautiful thing I've ever
suffered through,
ache like a
purple gown that trailed
behind me when I walked.

I was glowing, mother.
I was the most elegant
loneliness, the most exquisite
creature among all of the
unloved.

CHOCOLATE CHIP PANCAKES

You are making breakfast
in every dream that I have
of you.

You are in the kitchen, your
soft middle pressed up against
the cold marble countertops
like a vision too beautiful
for the magazines, sprinkling
dark chocolate chips
over pancakes.

I think for a brief second
that I am dreaming inside of my dream,
that I had to make you up twice,
just to get it right.

You, brushing your dark hair out
of your face, smearing batter
across your cheeks.

You have come and made
my visions smaller, warmer.
Filled them with sugar and
your body humming in the
same room as mine.

I wish, now, of a normal life
with you.

A life where breakfast lasts until
the sun goes down,
until I have finished gazing at
you from across
the table,

flour dried to your forehead
like a kiss.

LIVING GIRL

for Jewel

They say that you
remind them
of a deathbed.

A graveyard.

Dead girl, they call you.
The grim reaper.
The one who knows where
the bodies are buried but
can't say why.

They ask why your mouth
doesn't care about the living
anymore.

You, the one who watched
the world die, who could feel
the sword push through her,
the one touched
by a God that no one
can look in the eye.

Living girl.
Call yourself living girl.
You, with the bat in your hands,
with the voices in your head, with
the echoes, the mourning.
Breathing girl.
Darling girl.
Deathless
girl.

No one alive
can hurt you.

TICKET

You are a car parked
at the other end
of the theater,

a hand on the opposite side
of the cash register.

I used to keep the change
in my pocket until
it turned green
and filthy,
but now I pay in exact.

It's not you.
It's not you,
anymore.

SCISSORHANDS

She calls my arms a crime scene,
licks the blood from my chest,
then listens to the thumping
beneath it.

Yes, she knows what these
hands have done.

She knows I've poked holes
in the water of every bed
I've ever slept in,
knows what my heart
looks like when it's tired;
the pastel houses lining the streets.
The lipstick shades
of the bored housewives
with their ambrosia salads,
stuffing the mouth of pain until
it can't say their names anymore.

She loves me this many bodies-worth.
She loves me this many mountains.
She stretches across the room,
forgives me without blinking.

THROAT

I wanted to be a piece of
heaven that got stuck
in your throat.

I wanted a love like
holy water.

I wanted a bible that
remembered
me.

STREETLIGHT

God lives in the streetlight
outside of Nana's house,
a black clump in the center of him
made of bodies.

God is where
the moths go to die.
God ties
their wings together
to make them
bigger, plays with them
like a kid plays with dolls
in a horror movie.

Moths climb into the light
because they
think it's the moon,

because they love the moon
more than they love God
and he can't stand it.

I will never love anything that can swallow me.
I will never love anything that I can

fit inside of.

ACHILLES TO PATROCLUS

My love, how was I to know
that they would make a myth of us?
Did we not die? Are we not dead?
Are your bones not my bones?

Before the war.
Before we had to
kiss Troy out of each other's
teeth, we were a paradise.
You were the only one I kneeled
before.

You made the warrior in me tired.

They write about your death.
How I sliced through countless
men trying to build a
monument to the monster
I was after your body
blazed before me.

I can tell you now that
I begged for the arrow.
Welcomed it.
My last wish was to
sleep beside you in our tent.
To hide you so well in the afterlife
that no God could take you
from me again.

My quiet love was yours from the
beginning. I call my ankles
by your name.

When mother dipped me in the river,
she was introducing us.

PATROCLUS TO ACHILLES

On the night of my death,
your despair was so loud
that I could hear it
clawing through the earth to find me.
All the men screaming, begging,
still could not drown out the
wailing of your hands.

I once held your soldier heart
between my war teeth, shook it
like a dog with a bone until
it knew the fear of good love.
Do you remember?

I wore your armor
just to feel deathless.
I wore your armor just to know
what it meant to be inside of you.

I will dream of kissing your ankles again,
of pulling the weeping arrow out of you
and cutting through the earth
so that we may walk among it.

My love. My life.
What I would give to be
the only pile of ashes here.
What I would give to be
a sleeping body beside you.

THE RETURN

Persephone always brings
back a bouquet of roses
when she returns,
greets Hades with a long,
drawn out kiss.

She lets him bury
his Godhead in her black spring
locks while she dusts the soot
off of him.

The dead moan quietly in their
garden as Hades digs a new
hole for the flowers.

Persephone dances and her body
spins away from him.

He remembers what
her hair tastes like
when she leaves.

WASH

Love ended and there
was no music.

Not even
a violin.

All that was left was the
driveway where it happened
and the sock that they dropped
on their way not-home,
not-here, not-anymore.

It happens like that.
No one makes a plaque for the death
of a small love.

No one makes a statue for forgetting.
They just wander over the dirt
until the grass grows back.

So you wash the sock
and place it in your drawer
where it will find its way
into the pile of unmatched
ones and you'll wear it
one day without even
realizing.

You remember
but it doesn't
hurt
anymore.

ONE

I am not sorry
that I am not the
One.

I am not sorry
that the kiss wasn't enough,
that you go to a different bar
and wait for a different girl
every weekend.

I am not sorry that my staircase
was not the grand staircase,
that our dance was sweaty and sloppy
and in the dark.

I didn't want the movie fuck.

I didn't want the ball gown,
the silk underwear slowly pulled down my legs.
I didn't want the quiet sex,
the closed eyes open mouth *Dove* chocolate commercial sex.
I wanted it rough and honest and messy.

My bed was just a bed,
and you didn't know what
a good thing was when you
touched it.

Oh well.

I am the realest thing you've ever
forgotten about.

I am still
under your fingernails
when you bite them.

FINCH

I cried all over your poem
and ruined it.
Got dirt on the corner and
dragged my stupid feet
across it.

It was about a finch
that slept in the rafters
on your porch.
You were mad until it started
singing your favorite song.

In the end, it left with a bag
over its shoulder, and you
swore you never thought it
would.

That's how it works, though.
Nothing alive can stay
in one place for that long,
especially if you love it.

The finch was me.
I know that now.

I'm not sorry I left but
I'm sorry that I wanted to.

WHEN HANNA MET MARGARET

They ask Hanna if she knew
Margaret in a biblical sense,
and, well, yes but no.
Yes, they fucked,
but no, not biblically.
Her hand on Margaret's
body was not in the bible.
In fact, her hand on Margaret's
body came before the bible.

Her hand was invented
before God was, before
anything existed, before
the burning bush, before
all the men and their quests, their
blood.

Just a single hand in the desert,
made specifically for Margaret's
soft waist, soft cheeks, soft thighs.

She knew her prehistorically,
knew her anciently.

When their bodies met,
the earth got quiet again.

The continents held hands.

The comet fell limp in an unnamed river
and killed nothing,
smoke rising and disappearing
like a thing unremembered.

HONEY

She leaves his honey
on a small plate in the kitchen,
thinks about dipping her fingers in it
and writing
Come Back
on the granite counter tops
because leaving is sticky and tastes best
when licked off of the fingers or smeared
across the mouth.

He woke up and walked out the front door,
told her he couldn't sleep
then never came back.
Left his tea on the dining room table
like he would return for it.

No one really leaves
but they're always missed,
anyway.

WITH TEETH

You are bell bottom jeans and the sweater
your mom made you wear on the first
day of middle school.
You are the white bread Bologna sandwich
that you don't eat.
Half of Stacey's cold pizza lunchable, instead.

You are the year-long hunger
of eighth grade, the black eyeliner sadness.
You are the rumbling belly of thirteen.
You are the note on the ground,
the wrinkled shirt collar of the kid
who Adam beat up for you.

You are the heavy grey t-shirt
that you jump into the pool with.
The long walk back to your towel
when you climb out of the water.

You are an entire summer spent
with long sleeves on.
You are the sweat that never washes off,
the eyes closing for too long after
someone touches you.

You are the loneliness with teeth.
The one that bites back but never
has anything to bite.

A GOD EATS

Dreaming, now, of God eating
the sun.

His sun.

He unhinges his jaw, swallows
it whole like the serpent.

And then
there is no light.
Not a single
fire to be seen on any stretch of grass.

God eats the flames, too, wishing to
be bigger than the stories.

If I were a story, I'd be the one that
saves you when God comes to eat the
yellow star from your throat.

I'd be the
torch that sends him back to the blackness
that he wants to put inside of you.

I'd tell the darkness to keep its hands off of you.
Not because I own you but
because nothing does.

FLOWER BOY

A vision of you watering the
nasturtiums in the backyard.
The nozzle of the hose
looks nothing like a gun, and
you are not trying to hurt
anyone.

I used to wonder what the point of
daydreaming about you was if it wasn't frantic,
if I didn't want you even when you
were scary.

When I think about the kiss,
I remember that it didn't hurt,
that your bed was softer
than any floor I'd ever dreamed
of getting thrown on.

I don't think that love is what I grew up
pretending it was.

It's not angry.

It's not up against a wall all the time.

It's soft. It laughs.

RETURNING

Parts of you in the teeth,
in the tongue.

Parts of you in the leather
of the backseat,

in the fog
of the window.

The moon remembers you
only by
the smoothness of your back,

and therefore cannot
find you
unless you answer
your phone and come back
to the parking lot with me

so that she can see you again.

Okay, so I am lying
about the moon.

She wasn't looking
at you. I was the only
star staring.

You left your fingers in my hair
and I would only like

to give them

back to you.

PHILADELPHIA

She told me to write your
name down.

Instead, I dug out
a space for what you did
and carried it there, beneath
the stomach.

I put my hand over
the hollow and wondered
why you needed to be
remembered this badly.

You thought you were the kind of
nightmare that would stay with me forever,
the phantom that would never leave my body.

I wrote it down.
I wrote your name down
and you emptied out of me,
splattering onto the paper
like spilled soup.

It hurt but I did it.

The only ghost
you gave me
was the one
I killed.

WATER

The body wanted water
so it came to you
on its knees

and cried for three straight years
until the dirt was mud again.

When the grass returned
so did the gold
and the daisies.

There was singing again.
Drinking.

The body has forever
commemorated you
as the ender of the drought,

as the rain-giver.

The body
thanks you for the flood
and the flourishing– invites you
to wade knee-deep
into the miracle
and understand

why it was needed.

BIBLICAL

Call it the rapture
when someone
sees me naked
for the first
time.

The second coming.
Biblical the way all soft
women are biblical.

The New Testament begins
with the light switch flicking
on, my skin as an offering
placed gently
on the tongue. Melting.

The body as my body,
as my blood.
The thirst as the inevitable
thirst.

A week spent making
a New World to be kissed in,
to be banished from,
to wander in.

And on this day,
I walked out of the garden,
ran from the garden.

And on this day, I
created light.
I was light.
I was light.

CUT

You are
a better knife
than you are
a person.

Kiss like a blade to
a chopping block.

I catch you as you
sharpen and wonder
how you came to me.

ICE FISHING

I am touched only in
the places that he has
touched me.
The animal of my body
now hanging from
the hooks of his fingers.

He is gentle the way
all things are gentle.
The way
the gun is gentle after it has
gone through you for the last time.

He carves a circle around the heart
and waits for it.

He says,
Come,
let me show you
how to pull the bones out of a fish
without having to cut it open.

AS YOU WERE

I want to remember you
as you were
during the hurricane,

when the flood
made you raise your house
like a skirt over the knees.

Before the water, I was
inconsolable.
I was a door flung open
and kept open; a note
held until the voice
broke.

Your thunder shook me
with its hands in the
living room— kissed
my right temple
like it was exactly what it
was
until I stood still.

I remember the moment
I became moved,
how your body hummed
around me until my voice was void.

I was rocked silent
in the center of you.

Held quiet in the eye.

EAST CLAY AVENUE

He's gone.
Probably in Denver
or Minnesota or some other place
that isn't here, writing poems
about someone who isn't you.

Let him leave you for good, then.
For ever.
You're worth more than the dream
of him fucking you in the back
seat of his car,
your sweaty thighs
sticking to the seats.

Let that voicemail be the last
voicemail you leave for someone
who doesn't deserve it.

When he calls back,
and he will call back,
pretend that you don't
remember a thing.

HEAVY

I think about your voice on
the drive back home
and
how it echoed like a place
that everyone just left,
how it rang like a bell
in an empty church parking lot.

Your tongue made the candles cry,
blue flames dripping into the lake
and flooding it until
everything rose to the surface.

You are sadness with bones in it,
murky green water sadness.
Thick like a body,
heavy like a phone call.

MIRRORS

1.
Looking at my reflection too much.
Sitting in the back seat
of the car and gazing at myself
in the rear view mirror.

My dad tells me that I look fine
and to stop staring at myself
while he's driving.

I reapply my lipstick, watch myself
do it in the black
screen of my iPhone.
Someone on this bus thinks
I'm the most conceited person
who has ever lived.

I bite my lips while my professor
is talking,
imagine giving him a hand-job
during his office hours while
he tells me how pretty I am.

I'm in the reflection of his glasses,
of the laptop on his desk, of the
shiny gold band around his finger.
He's not even looking.

2.
A funhouse mirror.
My body a lava lamp of ugly shapes.

Everyone laughs at the one
that makes their stomachs stretch.
I laugh at the one that makes me
look like a lamp post.

The stranger next to me has hair
down to her hips and I can't

see anything except for her earth body
and my little streetlight one.

We turn away from
the mirror and I snap back into
the globe of myself, thinking

Who could hold the whole world?
Who would even want to?

I'd let her touch me, if she asked.
I'd live in the funhouse
if it meant I could be
small enough for her
to wrap her arms
around.

3.
Her eyes, mirrors.
I'm a panoramic
in the gloss of them.

She's looking right
at me.

EDEN

I want to die without
dying.

I want the knowledge that
comes with dying– the fruit
of the labor.

The proof that someone
was watching.

I want to unhook my shadow
from the wall and dress it in
street clothes.

Not quite a dead thing but
almost.

The echo that knows
what it means
to leave

and then come back.

FRUIT

Each day you are
peeled back and eaten.
Not like Prometheus
on the hill but
like an orange.

You are person
and not an orange
but I still think
you're good for me the way
an orange is good for me.

The way I eat it with my hands.

When you love someone
you lick your fingers more.
No one knows why.
Or maybe they do
and they just don't want
to say.

I wish I knew.

I wish we could peel together.
Eat the fruit together.

That's what it all
comes down to,
anyway.

Sharing the orange.

Eating the rind.

MOTEL

A motel for
the secret of you.
Sweaty hands
on the back,
on the weight
of her.

She only wanted to travel
to get out of her body
but she is in Colorado now
and you're touching her.

A cigarette for
the afterwards, like the movies.

You shower in the rusty bathroom
and think about leaving
because she told you
not to tell her your name.

It's never simple.
Crying love after one night
but also not crying love.

Keeping it quiet because
it's not even
a word in your mouth yet.

Marbles for your tongue
when you see her asleep
in the bed that belongs
to neither of you.

Because there's nothing
to say. Nothing to do now.
No going anywhere
except with
her.

LOCKED

I am up nights
thinking about what
I could have done
to close the gates sooner.

I saw your body as it tried
to slip through the iron bars.

I saw your hands, your fingers
reaching through, your white
teeth patches of neon
in the moonlight.

You said you loved me but it felt like being robbed.
Your smile was twisted like the metal rose
on the lock you couldn't pick.

You didn't get in but you
got close. Your hands
almost pulled me out
of the house, into the car
that I never want to see again.

When I say I'll never forget you
I do not mean it kindly.

CLUB BOYS

It's always at clubs. They keep
their distance, wait for your
body to sway into theirs just
once and then they don't
ask you again if they can put
their hands there or if they
can sit down next to you.

Your neck is some couch in a dark corner
where they don't think anything counts.
They don't ask any questions.
They're land mines that you
try to dance around
but they explode anyway, always.

And you just came to dance,
to drink, to look pretty with your friends.
And they have to come and touch you
when you don't want them to.
And they have to make you afraid.
And they make a body a war,
a body a secret,
a tragedy.

And they leave you in the bathroom.
And they don't even look you in the eye
when they do it.

FORGOTTEN

I have not forgotten you.
Your sad scent, your
wild hair, wild eyes,
your sharp upper lip.

I have not forgotten.
When you find me again,
you will find yourself
remembered, revered,
thought of often.

Even if I don't love you like I did,
you won't be a stranger.
You could never be a stranger.

Some people look just as familiar
walking away as they do walking back,
and I am so fond of your spine
in that brown coat.

I have not forgotten.
I have not
forgotten.

MYTH

There is no difference between
a God and a Hungry God.

If you do not feed them
what you have killed, they will eat
their own heart, down to
the fingers.

The myth is that love was
invented by them.
The sister of the open mouth,
they thought.

Love was a drop of rain that fell
from the stomach of their sky.

A mistake.
A gift from no one
and they have been empty
ever since.

The Gods do not go hungry
because they are always

hungry.

They never die because they are
already dead.

APPETITE

To think that love and love alone
could mend us. Feed us.

To think that love alone
could carry a broken body
out of a burning room.

If we are hungry then we are
hungry for food, hungry for
the water, for the sun.

If we
are hungry at all,
it is not
for a body,

it is not for
each other.

CORNER

Death likes being in the room
when the babies are born.
Not because she has to be, but
because she doesn't have to be.
Not usually.

Death likes to stand in the corner
like a pimply kid at the high school
dance, likes to sway quietly behind
the bleachers while the whole room
gets kissed.

Death likes to watch the worlds
that don't need her, likes to haunt
alleyways like the most forgotten
spirit in all of Manhattan.

I like the way you look after you've seen her.
After she leaves her perfume
on your mouth.

If you ever loved me back, I think
it would have ruined it. No one
actually touches death.

I'd be a ghost in the hall outside
the room that you kiss her in.

EVERYWHERE EXCEPT

Here is the true story.

You saw a beautiful boy and
it fucked you up.

You saw a beautiful boy and
you thought you could have him,
so you waited like something
empty waits to be filled.

He is the greedy water around
your drowning car,

the hand around your waist.

He is the stray that won't come inside,

the night around the moon.

He is everywhere except
inside of you.

HANDY GUIDE TO NAVIGATING THE FANTASY

STEP ONE: never enjoy The Fantasy for too long.
Leave enough time to recover, to remember
your small bed.

STEP TWO: never engage with The Fantasy.
Cross the street every time.
In case of an emergency, you can hug them outside
of the movie theater, but try not to.

STEP THREE: tell no one about The Fantasy.
It will disappear if you do.

STEP FOUR: hold your death wish away from the body
after you see The Fantasy kiss a real person who isn't you.

STEP FIVE: suffer for how much of them you invented.
Crawl to the house you built for the two of you and suffer in it.

STEP FIVE: drop the death wish into your neighbor's garbage can.
Wash hands thoroughly.

STEP SIX: it hurts worse when it isn't real.
Write this on the ceiling.

STEP SEVEN: do not go back for the death wish. Do not go back.

MOTH

Imagine your girl as a moth
a fluttery thing with wings

and she keeps bumping into you
because you're the light on the porch,
the light in the shower,
the moon.
Something warm that she wants to
crawl inside of.
The hell of it is
you want her to.
You carve out a space below your belly button
and you let her press her face
against it, so different from
the last time you did this.

Maybe it's love when the wound
heals clean,

when she can't fly but you swear
you saw her once.

UNBURIED

Back again. Bones above ground.
Wind chime fingers in my hair.
A quiet knife-tongue on my shoulder.

An ancient ruin. Your teeth
the twenty eight steps
to the broken temple.
Fuck you. Fuck me. Eat
my palm. Eat my offering.
Climb down. Climb back.

I don't want to make sense
to anything, I just want to be
the stone you grind into powder.

Love, my violent myth, my
terrifying air.

Turn my water to wine. Eat
my heart out. Feed it to the sun.

Back again. Back again.
Unburied. Unburied and
pale. Dirt under my fingernails
because I like saving you.

Love, my angry body weeping.
Your sleeping mouth tattooed
on my sternum.
Love, my vicious secret.
Love, my hungry dream.

THE HANDS

Not so much the hands as what
one does with them.

Maya uses hers to braid her hair,
a soft ache in her arms by the time
she has finished.

Not so much the hands as what
fruit one peels.
Clementine. Grapefruit.
Pomegranate.
Hands to lips. Not so much
the hands as the feeding.
Maya kisses her mother
with that mouth,
leaves a trail of citrus behind her.

Not so much the hands
as the hunger.

Two open palms. Eager teeth.
A birthday cake and a boy's eyes
on her blue dress.

The hands and the feast.
She sits at a table and knows
what love looks like when
it has just eaten.
Fruit dripping
from the tongue
like spit from
a rabid dog.

HEAVEN IS

Heaven is
a pretty girl,

is her perfume
on the pillows,

is her mouth touching
your mouth,
is the fearless way
she kisses your collarbone.

Heaven is
her chia seeds
on your counter,
is her almond milk
in the fridge,

is her mug next to yours,
is her lipstick
on your belly,
on your neck,
on your teeth.

Heaven
is her body
when it is not
leaving your body,

when it is not leaving
at all.

STAY

Poetry about teeth
in a jar, cicada wings
in a jar,
dead and dying things
in jars that we keep
on our dressers.

An ant carried another
dead ant on its back all the way
across your room and into
the small hole in the wall.

Your teeth rattle on the wood counter
during the storm.
The cicadas latch onto your windows
And peel away like a second skin.

That picture you don't need
anymore
stands straight-spined
on the table by the bed.

When you lose something
you keep it with you.
It stays.

RUMINATION

Always the loneliest one
in the room, now.
Always gnawing
at the bones of love,
of hot wings, because
the meat isn't enough,
you need it
to sting.

Always the hungriest
one in the bed,
at the table.
Always asking for seconds,
for more, licking your fingers
because you're shameless
when you're not alone.

If love could fit inside you
it would eat you
from the inside out.
Hunger eating hunger
until you're just
a girl again.

You are not the only survivor
of the empty stomach, but
you are the only one
who survived
in this particular way.

No one else knows what you do
when no one wants what you
have.

No one else loves a hand
with something in it
as much as you do.

AIRPORT

She never goes where she is wanted
and you can smell it on her when she
walks through the door of the bar.

All packed suitcase, all
car air freshener
all airplane food and alcohol.

She smells like running towards a flood
instead of away from it,
wading up to the waist and then
drowning.

A cataclysm of a person, burying
every place that wouldn't keep her
because what else can she do.

You wonder what she's like when
she's tired, when she's not leaving,
if running really is so special
that it's worth
dying
for.

DEATH MARCH

You with your death march
and your death wish
and your love poems.

I can't keep up with the violence
he wakes in you,
can't keep up with which story
is the real story about what happened
when you two kissed
and it ruined everything.

What happened after you didn't want
to die anymore?

After all of this
wasn't a fist shoved
in your mouth
trying to pull him out?

You said the word love
like it was a dirge
at your own funeral,

like it could pull
you out of a grave
and then put you
back in it.

He can't save you
better than you do.

BURNING

Love, you said, was a fire
outside the door of a place
you don't want to be anymore.

An ambulance waiting
around the corner.

I pictured the cathedral of you
going up in flames, then,
the holy dresser melting your
holy clothes.
Every inch of the blessed bed orange and
angry.

I swear I'll survive every fire
after this one.
I'll walk out of every house
I ever missed you in
and let the smoke eat the doorways.

I'll write on the walls:

You are sacred because
I have made you sacred.
There is no burning that I
did not create.

THE GARDEN

What would he say if he knew
that she bit the snake before
she ever bit the apple.

What would he say if he knew
what it really tasted like.

She swears it wasn't about the knowledge
so much as the fear of not having it.
She didn't even want to write down,
that it was his holy fault,

that no harm should come to
the girl who got hungry in the room
that he locked her in.

Because she may have listened
to the serpent
but he's the one who let it
into the garden.

LOVELESS

In the dream that matters
I have nowhere to be.
I have four dogs who sleep
in the bed with me, and I can
drink coffee again
without getting
sick.

I always talk about love
but I've seen a life
where I can live without it,
where I can eat with my hands,
make the whole bed,
and leave the light on
for myself.

ABOUT THE AUTHOR

Caitlyn Siehl is a 22 year old poet living in New Jersey. She is currently attending graduate school at Rutgers University. She has coedited two anthologies and published her first full length poetry book, *What We Buried*, in 2014 with Words Dance Publishing. Her work has also been published on *Thought Catalog*, in the *Rising Phoenix Review*, and *Hooligan Magazine*.

GRATITUDES

To everyone who reads this book. Friends, strangers, family, so on and so forth. You have changed my life just by supporting me and my work. I am forever grateful for your faith in me. Let's run off into the sunset together.

To Amanda Oaks, for being the best damn publisher and person I've ever known. Your loveliness knows no bounds. I owe all of this to you.

To women everywhere. To the crybabies, to the stone angels. I see you. Thank you.

WORDS DANCE PUBLISHING has one aim:

To spread mind-blowing / heart-opening poetry.

Words Dance artfully & carefully wrangles words that were born to dance wildly in the heart-mind matrix. Rich, edgy, raw, emotionally-charged energy balled up & waiting to whip your eyes wild; we rally together words that were written to make your heart go boom right before they slay your mind.

Words Dance Publishing is an independent press out of Pennsylvania. We work closely & collaboratively with all of our writers to ensure that their words continue to breathe in a sound & stunning home. Most importantly though, we leave the windows in these homes unlocked so you, the reader, can crawl in & throw one fuck of a house party.

To learn more about our books, authors, events & Words Dance Poetry Magazine, visit:

WORDSDANCE.COM

Why I'm Not Where You Are by Brianna Albers

The Goddess Songs by Azra Tabassum

No Matter the Time by Fortesa Latifi

Before the First Kiss by Ashe Vernon & Trista Mateer

Our Bodies & Other Fine Machines by Natalie Wee

holyFool by Amanda Oaks

A FIELD OF BLOOMING BRUISES
Poetry by Schuyler Peck

| $12 | 58 pages | 5.5" x 8.5" | softcover |

ISBN: 978-0692628591

To my first year of recovery, my first impression was wrong, you turned out much sweeter than I thought. To my followers, who inspire me daily with their kindness; for all the friends I haven't met yet. To my friends, you are every light I've ever looked for. To my Tyler, for giving me enough love, I can fill books with it.

"Peck's poems carry both a lovely fragility and a sense of strength, and it is a testament to her prowess as a poet that she comes out of her trials all that much stronger because of it. While some poems here are stronger than others, nothing here is boring or ordinary. There is a warmth to Peck's words, and she wears her soft nature with no sense of shame. You could lump her in with similar poets like Clementine Von Radics and Charlotte Erikkson, but she's better than both of them, and has the potential to be one of the best contemporary poets, in time."

— **KENDALL A. BELL**
Publisher/Editor @ *Maverick Duck Press*

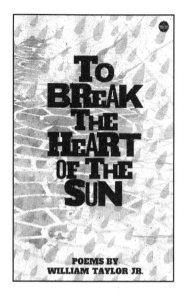

TO BREAK THE HEART OF THE SUN
Poetry by William Taylor Jr.

| $15 | 132 pages | 5.5" x 8.5" | softcover |

ISBN: 978-0692617380

"*In To Break the Heart of the Sun* Taylor invites you over for a few drinks & then takes you out on the gritty streets of San Francisco. You dip into the bars & cafés in the Tenderloin & North Beach, you skirt the sidewalks down Haight, in Chinatown & the Mission, all the while bonding over the people you love, music, poetry, past loves, friendship, your childhoods & dreams. You question life, both the dark & light of it, looking for the truth of it. You laugh & weep with the people you meet along the way, every face some kind of prayer. Taylor teaches you how to dance with your joy while dressed in your sorrow. He has a way of showing you how keep your heart open & closed at the same time so you don't lose your footing, but if you do, with kind eyes & laughter escaping both your lips, his hand reaches down to help you up."

"William Taylor, Jr, my pick for best poet in San Francisco, is back with *To Break the Heart of the Sun*, and it's every bit a Taylor book, every bit as sad, and beautiful, and even begrudgingly hopeful as all his best work. Or, if not hopeful, that at least graceful in its wise and simple acceptance of the silly problem called life. His lines crackle and sing, sweeping through the crumbling landscape of the Tenderloin, and the vast, Buddha-like landscape of his inner life. These poems will save something otherwise lost even as we fumbling, stuttering mortals fade...and I can think of no higher honor than that. And Amanda at Words Dance has put together a drop-dead gorgeous book, with cover-art on par with those sublime Black Sparrow covers of years past...so there is absolutely nothing but praise for this entire glorious project. Treat yourself to a copy!"

— **HOSHO MCCREESH**
Author of *A Deep and Gorgeous Thirst*

Other titles available from
WORDS DANCE PUBLISHING

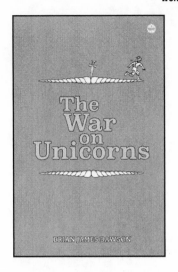

THE WAR ON UNICORNS
Poetry by Brian James Dawson

| $12 | 74 pages | 5.5" x 8.5" | softcover |

ISBN: 978-0692487754

"*The War on Unicorns*, with its parts 1 through 40, which from its opening lines- *The dog barks constantly. Shining men in / riot gear accept flowers.* – enters the conflicting imaginations of the local and the empyreal. The book itself is a halcyonian triumph. Lines, of course, abound. *A paper airplane flies towards a furnace* (2). *A remade red dress / hangs lugubriously on a wooden rack / in a closet left over from / the Mormon migration* (5). But I've said too much of what it merely says. It doesn't build, it contains, it is house. Inside, there is map enough to distract the bombings. At one point, Dawson directs us to *Remember Tehran*. It is not jarring, it is just the end of a poem. Dawson is a student of history but teaches the sane myth."

— **BARTON SMOCK**
Author of *Misreckon* & *The Blood You Don't See Is Fake*

"The poems in *The War on Unicorns* are perfect examples of the best words in the best order. I love the snap-shot feel of each poem, and if a picture is worth a thousand words, then these word-pictures are golden. *Piles/of old newspapers /yellow in the long light/of a sequester sun* and *he wishes-wishes to retract all his lies / and rake them into multi-colored piles.* The observation of human experiences and relationships are sharp - *I am the curator of the universe's / museum of cruel jokes.* This writing has both style and substance. *Take off your armor; unlock your heart* - you should buy this book."

— **VIOLET WILD**

WHAT WE BURIED
Poetry by Caitlyn Siehl

| $12 | 64 pages | 5.5" x 8.5" | softcover |

ISBN: 978-0615985862

GOODREADS CHOICE AWARD NOMINEE FOR POETRY (2014)

This book is a cemetery of truths buried alive. The light draws you in where you will find Caitlyn there digging. When you get close enough, she'll lean in & whisper, Baby, buried things will surface no matter what, get to them before they get to you first. Her unbounded love will propel you to pick up a shovel & help— even though the only thing you want to do is kiss her lips, kiss her hands, kiss every one of her stretch marks & the fire that is raging in pit of her stomach. She'll see your eyes made of devour & sadness, she'll hug you & say, Baby, if you eat me alive, I will cut my way out of your stomach. Don't let this be your funeral. Teach yourself to navigate the wound.

"It takes a true poet to write of love and desire in a way that manages to surprise and excite. Caitlyn Siehl does this in poem after poem and makes it seem effortless. Her work shines with a richness of language and basks in images that continue to delight and astound with multiple readings. *What We Buried* is a treasure from cover to cover."

— **WILLIAM TAYLOR JR.**
Author of *An Age of Monsters*

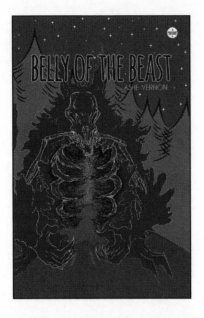

BELLY OF THE BEAST
Poetry by Ashe Vernon

| $12 | 82 pages | 5.5" x 8.5" | softcover |

ISBN: 978-0692300541

"Into the *Belly of the Beast* we crawl with Ashe as our guide; into the dark visceral spaces where love, lust, descent and desire work their transformative magic and we find ourselves utterly altered in the reading. A truly gifted poet and truth-spiller, Ashe's metaphors create images within images, leading us to question the subjective truths, both shared and hidden, in personal relationship — to the other, and to oneself. Unflinching in her approach, her poetry gives voice to that which most struggle to admit — even if only to themselves. And as such, *Belly of the Beast* is a work of startling courage and rich depth — a darkly delicious pleasure."

— AMY PALKO
Goddess Guide, Digital Priestess & Writer

"It isn't often you find a book of poetry that is as unapologetic, as violent, as moving as this one. Ashe's writing is intense and visceral. You feel the punch in your gut while you're reading, but you don't question it. You know why it's there and you almost welcome it."

— CAITLYN SIEHL
Author of *What We Buried*

"The poems you are about to encounter are the fierce time capsules of girl-hood, girded with sharp elbows, surprise kisses, the meanders of wander-lust. We need voices this strong, this true for the singing reminds us that we are not alone, that someone, somewhere is listening for the faint pulse that is our wish to be seen. Grab hold, this voice will be with us forever."

— RA WASHINGTON
GuidetoKulchurCleveland.com

Other titles available from
WORDS DANCE PUBLISHING

DOWRY MEAT

Poetry by Heather Knox

| $12 | 110 pages | 5.5" x 8.5" | softcover |

ISBN: 978-0692398494

Heather Knox's *Dowry Meat* is a gorgeous, tough-as-nails debut that arrives on your doorstep hungry and full of dark news. There's damage here, and obsession, and more haunted beauty in the wreckage of just about everything—relationships, apartment clutter, rough sex, the body, and of course the just-post apocalypse—than you or I could hope to find on our own. These are poems that remind us not that life is hard—that's old news—but that down there in the gravel and broken glass is where the truth-worth-hearing lies, and maybe the life worth living. If you were a city, Knox tells us, unflinching as always, *I'd... read your graffiti. Drink your tap water./Feel your smog and dirt stick to my sweat... If you were a city, I'd expect to be robbed.*

— **JON LOOMIS**

Author of *Vanitas Motel (winner of the FIELD prize)* and *The Pleasure Principle*

"Heather Knox's debut collection is a lyric wreath made of purulent ribbon and the most inviting of thorns. Tansy and tokophobia, lachrymosity and lavage are braided together in this double collection, which marries a sci-fi Western narrative to a lyric sequence. Both elapse in an impossible location made of opposites—futuristic nostalgia, or erotic displeasure—otherwise known as the universe in which we (attempt to) live."

— **JOYELLE MCSWEENEY**

Author of *The Necropastoral: Poetry, Media, Occults & Salamandrine: 8 Gothics*

"*Dowry Meat*'s apocalyptic fever dream myth-making bleeds into what we might call the poetry of witness or the tradition of the confessional, except that these lines throb with lived experience and a body isn't necessarily a confession. Heather Knox's poems are beautifully wrought and beautifully raw."

— **DORA MALECH**

Author of *Shore Ordered Ocean & Say So*

THE NO YOU NEVER LISTENED TO
Poetry by Meggie Royer

| $14 | 142 pages | 5.5" x 8.5" | softcover |

ISBN: 978-0692463635

"It's a strange thing when the highest praise you can offer for someone's work is, "I wish this didn't exist," but that was the refrain that echoed in my head after I read Meggie Royer's third book.

As fans of her work know, Meggie takes the universal and makes it personal. With *The No You Never Listened To*, she takes the personal and makes it universal. As a sexual assault survivor, Meggie is well-acquainted with trauma: the aftermath, the guilt, the anger. She has never shied away from taking Hemingway's advice – write hard and clear about what hurts – and that strength has never been more of an asset than with this body of work.

The No You Never Listened To is the book you will wish you'd had when trauma climbed into your bed. It is the book you will give to friends who are dragged from their "before" into a dark and terrifying "after". And yes, it is the book you will wish didn't exist.

But it is also the one that will remind you, in your darkest moments, where the blame really belongs. It will remind you that your memory will not always be an enemy. And it will remind you that none of us have ever been alone in this."

— **CLAIRE BIGGS**

To Write Love on Her Arms Editor / Writer

"Nietzsche once warned us to be careful gazing into the abyss, that we run the risk of staring so long that the void consumes us. The poems in this book were born of the abyss, of conflict & trauma & survival. And through these poems, Meggie Royer stares – hard, unflinching, courageous – and instead of gazing back, the abyss looks away."

— **WILLIAM JAMES**

Drunk In A Midnight Choir editor & author of rebel hearts & restless ghosts

CHLOE

Poetry by Kristina Haynes

| $12 | 110 pages | 5.5" x 8.5" | softcover |

ISBN: 978-0692386637

Chloe is brave and raw, adolescence mixed with salt. These poems are about how hungry we've been, how foolish, how lonely. Chloe is not quite girl nor woman, full of awkward bravery. Kristina is an electric voice that pulls Chloe apart page after page, her heartbreaks, her too many drinks, her romantic experiences of pleasure and pain. Chloe and Kristina make a perfect team to form an anthem for girls everywhere, an anthem that reassures us we deserve to take up space. Indeed, when I met Chloe, I too thought "This is the closest I've been to anybody in months."

— **MEGGIE ROYER**

Author of *Survival Songs*
and *Healing Old Wounds with New Stitches*

"*Chloe* is one of the most intimate books you'll read all year. Chloe is my new best friend. I want to eat burnt popcorn on her couch and watch Friends reruns. I want to borrow her clothing, write on her walls in lipstick. Chloe is not your dream girl. She doesn't have everything figured out. She's messy. She's always late. She promises old lovers she'll never call again. She teaches you what the word "indulgence" means. She's wonderful, wonderful, wonderful. In *Chloe*, Kristina Haynes digs into the grittiness of modern womanhood, of mothers and confusion and iPhones and two, maybe three-night-stands. Her truths are caramels on the tongue but are blunter, harsher on the way down. Kristina introduces us to a character I'll be thinking about for a very long time. Go read this book. Then write a poem. Then kiss someone. Then buy an expensive strain of tea and a new pillow. Then go read it again."

— **YASMIN BELKHYR**

Editor-in-Chief at *Winter Tangerine Review*

LITERARY SEXTS
VOLUME 2

A Collection of Short & Sexy Love Poems

| $12 | 76 pages | 5.5" x 8.5" | softcover |

ISBN: 978-0692359594

This is the highly anticipated second volume of Literary Sexts! After over 1,000 copies of Literary Sexts Volume 1 being sold, we are super-excited to bring you a second volume! Literary Sexts is an annual modern day anthology of short love & sexy poems edited by Amanda Oaks & Caitlyn Siehl. These are poems that you would text to your lover. Poems that you would slip into a back pocket, suitcase, wallet or purse on the sly. Poems that you would write on slips of paper & stick under your crush's windshield wiper or pillow. Poems that you would write on a Post-it note & leave on the bathroom mirror. Poems that you would whisper into your lover's ear. Hovering around 40 contributors & 130 poems, this book reads is like one long & very intense conversation between two lovers. It's absolutely breathtaking.

This is for the leather
& the lace of you–

your flushed cheeks
& what set them ablaze.

POEM YOUR HEART OUT
Prompts, Poems & Room to Add Your Own
Volume 1

| $15 | 158 pages | 5.5" x 8.5" | softcover |

ISBN: 978-0692317464

PROMPT BOOK • ANTHOLOGY • WORKBOOK

Words Dance Publishing teamed up with the Writer's Digest's Poetic Asides blog to make their Poem-A-Day challenge this year even more spectacular!

Part poetry prompt book, part anthology of the best poems written during the 2014 April PAD(Poem-A-Day) Challenge on the Poetic Asides blog (by way of Writer's Digest) & part workbook, let both, the prompt & poem, inspire you to create your own poetic masterpieces. Maybe you participated in April & want to document your efforts during the month. Maybe you're starting now, like so many before you, with just a prompt, an example poem, & an invitation to poem your heart out! You're encouraged—heck, dared—to write your own poems inside of this book!

This book is sectioned off by Days, each section will hold the prompt for that day, the winning poem for that day & space for you to place the poem you wrote for that day's prompt inside.

Just a few of the guest judges: Amy King, Bob Hicok, Jericho Brown, Nate Pritts, Kristina Marie Darling & Nin Andrews...

Challenge yourself, your friend, a writing workshop or your class to this 30 Day Poem-A-Day Challenge!

THIS IS AN INVITATION TO POEM YOUR HEART OUT!

I EAT CROW + BLUE COLLAR AT BEST
Poetry by Amanda Oaks + Zach Fishel

| \$15 | 124 pages | 5.5" x 8.5" | softcover |

Home is where the heart is and both poets' hearts were raised in the Appalachian region of Western Pennsylvania surrounded by coal mines, sawmills, two-bit hotel taverns, farms, churches and cemeteries. These poems take that region by the throat and shake it until it's bloody and then, they breathe it back to life. This book is where you go when you're looking for nostalgia to kick you in the teeth. This is where you go when you're 200 miles away from a town you thought you'd never want to return to but suddenly you're pining for it.

Amanda and Zach grew up 30 miles from each other and met as adults through poetry. Explore both the male and female perspective of what it's like to grow up hemmed in by an area's economic struggle. These poems mine through life, love, longing and death, they're for home and away, and the inner strength that is not deterred by any of those things.

SPLIT BOOK #1

What are Split Books?

Two full-length books from two poets in one + there's a collaborative split between the poets in the middle!

COLLECT THEM ALL!

SHAKING THE TREES
Poetry by Azra Tabassum

| $12 | 72 pages | 5.5" x 8.5" | softcover |

ISBN: 978-0692232408

From the very first page *Shaking the Trees* meets you at the edge of the forest, extends a limb & seduces you into taking a walk through the dark & light of connection. Suddenly, like a gunshot in the very-near distance, you find yourself traipsing though a full-blown love story that you can't find your way out of because the story is actually the landscape underneath your feet. It's okay though, you won't get lost– you won't go hungry. Azra shakes every tree along the way so their fruit blankets the ground before you. She picks up pieces & hands them to you but not before she shows you how she can love you so gently it will feel like she's unpeeling you carefully from yourself. She tells you that it isn't about the bite but the warm juice that slips from the lips down chin. She holds your hand when you're trudging through the messier parts, shoes getting stuck in the muck of it all, but you'll keep going with the pulp of the fruit still stuck in-between your teeth, the juice will dry in the crooks of your elbows & in the lines on your palms. You'll taste bittersweet for days.

"I honestly haven't read a collection like this before, or at least I can't remember having read one. My heart was wrecked by Azra. It's like that opening line in Fahrenheit 451 when Bradbury says, "It was a pleasure to burn." It really was a pleasure being wrecked by it."

— **NOURA**
of *NouraReads*

"I wanted to cry and cheer and fuck. I wanted to take the next person I saw and kiss them straight on the lips and say, "Remember this moment for the rest of your life."

— **CHELSEA MILLER**

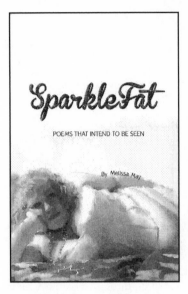

SPARKLEFAT

Poetry by Melissa May

| $12 | 62 pages | 5.5" x 8.5" | softcover |

SparkleFat is a loud, unapologetic, intentional book of poetry about my body, about your body, about fat bodies and how they move through the world in every bit of their flash and spark and burst. Some of the poems are painful, some are raucous celebrations, some are reminders and love letters and quiet gifts back to the vessel that has traveled me so gracefully - some are a hymnal of yes, but all of them sparkle. All of them don't mind if you look – really. They built their own house of intention, and they draped that shit in lime green sequins. All of them intend to be seen. All of them have no more fucks to give about a world that wants them to be quiet.

"I didn't know how much I needed this book until I found myself, three pages in, ugly crying on the plane next to a concerned looking business man. This book is the most glorious, glittery pink permission slip. It made me want to go on a scavenger hunt for every speck of shame in my body and sing hot, sweaty R&B songs to it. There is no voice more authentic, generous and resounding than Melissa May. From her writing, to her performance, to her role in the community she delivers fierce integrity & staggering passion. From the first time I watched her nervously step to the mic, to the last time she crushed me in a slam, it is has been an honor to watch her astound the poetry slam world and inspire us all to be not just better writers but better people. We need her."

— LAUREN ZUNIGA
Author of *The Smell of Good Mud*

"*SparkleFat* is a firework display of un-shame. Melissa May's work celebrates all of the things we have been so long told deserved no streamers. This collection invites every fat body out to the dance and steams up the windows in the backseat of the car afterwards by kissing the spots we thought (or even hoped) no one noticed but are deserving of love just the same as our mouths."

— RACHEL WILEY
Author of *Fat Girl Finishing School*

Other titles available from
WORDS DANCE PUBLISHING

LOVE AND OTHER SMALL WARS

Poetry by Donna-Marie Riley

| $12 | 76 pages | 5.5" x 8.5" | softcover |

ISBN: 978-0615931111

Love and Other Small Wars reminds us that when you come back from combat usually the most fatal of wounds are not visible. Riley's debut collection is an arsenal of deeply personal poems that embody an intensity that is truly impressive yet their hands are tender. She enlists you. She gives you camouflage & a pair of boots so you can stay the course through the minefield of her heart. You will track the lovely flow of her soft yet fierce voice through a jungle of powerful imagery on womanhood, relationships, family, grief, sexuality & love, amidst other matters. Battles with the heart aren't easily won but Riley hits every mark. You'll be relieved that you're on the same side. Much like war, you'll come back from this book changed.

"Riley's work is wise, intense, affecting, and uniquely crafted. This collection illuminates her ability to write with both a gentle hand and a bold spirit. She inspires her readers and creates an indelible need inside of them to consume more of her exceptional poetry. I could read *Love and Other Small Wars* all day long…and I did."

— **APRIL MICHELLE BRATTEN**
editor of *Up the Staircase Quarterly*

"Riley's poems are personal, lyrical and so vibrant they practically leap off the page, which also makes them terrifying at times. A beautiful debut."

— **BIANCA STEWART**

LITERARY SEXTS

A Collection of Short & Sexy Love Poems
(Volume 1)

| $12 | 42 pages | 5.5" x 8.5" | softcover |

ISBN: 978-0615959726

Literary Sexts is a modern day anthology of short love poems with subtle erotic undertones edited by Amanda Oaks & Caitlyn Siehl. Hovering around 50 contributors & 124 poems, this book reads is like one long & very intense conversation between two lovers. It's absolutely breathtaking. These are poems that you would text to your lover. Poems that you would slip into a back pocket, suitcase, wallet or purse on the sly. Poems that you would write on slips of paper & stick under your crush's windshield wiper. Poems that you would write on a Post-it note & leave on the bathroom mirror.

HIT #1
ON AMAZON'S
HOT NEW
RELEASE LIST!

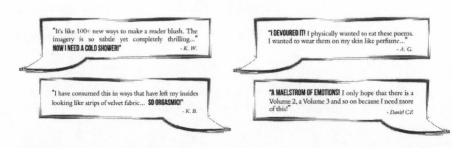

"It's like 100+ new ways to make a reader blush. The imagery is so subtle yet completely thrilling..." **NOW I NEED A COLD SHOWER!"**
- K. W.

"**I DEVOURED IT!** I physically wanted to eat these poems. I wanted to wear them on my skin like perfume..."
- A. G.

"I have consumed this in ways that have left my insides looking like strips of velvet fabric... **SO ORGASMIC!"**
- K. B.

"**A MAELSTROM OF EMOTIONS!** I only hope that there is a Volume 2, a Volume 3 and so on because I need more of this!"
- Daniel CZ

Other titles available from
WORDS DANCE PUBLISHING

a poem by kris ryan

Unrequited love? We've all been there.

Enter:

WHAT TO DO AFTER SHE SAYS NO
by Kris Ryan.

This skillfully designed 10-part poem explores what it's like to ache for someone. This is the book you buy yourself or a friend when you are going through a breakup or a one-sided crush, it's the perfect balance between aha, humor & heartbreak.

WHAT TO DO AFTER SHE SAYS NO
A Poem by Kris Ryan

$10 | 104 pages | 5" x 8" | softcover | ISBN: 978-0615870045

"*What to Do After She Says No* takes us from Shanghai to the interior of a refrigerator, but mostly dwells inside the injured human heart, exploring the aftermath of emotional betrayal. This poem is a compact blast of brutality, with such instructions as "Climb onto the roof and jump off. If you break your leg, you are awake. If you land without injury, pinch and twist at your arm until you wake up." Ryan's use of the imperative often leads us to a reality where pain is the only outcome, but this piece is not without tenderness, and certainly not without play, with sounds and images ricocheting off each other throughout. Anticipate the poetry you wish you knew about during your last bad breakup; this poem offers a first "foothold to climb out" from that universal experience."

— LISA MANGINI

"Reading Kris Ryan's *What To Do After She Says No* is like watching your heart pound outside of your chest. Both an unsettling visual experience and a hurricane of sadness and rebirth—this book demands more than just your attention, it takes a little bit of your soul, and in the end, makes everything feel whole again."

— JOHN DORSEY
author of *Tombstone Factory*

"*What to Do After She Says No* is exquisite. Truly, perfectly exquisite. It pulls you in on a familiar and wild ride of a heart blown open and a mind twisting in an effort to figure it all out. It's raw and vibrant...and in the same breath comforting. I want to crawl inside this book and live in a world where heartache is expressed so magnificently.

— JO ANNA ROTHMAN
MA, Coach & Conjurer of Electric Creative Wholeness

Tammy Foster Brewer is the type of poet who makes me wish I could write poetry instead of novels. From motherhood to love to work, Tammy's poems highlight the extraordinary in the ordinary and leave the reader wondering how he did not notice what was underneath all along. I first heard Tammy read 'The Problem is with Semantics' months ago, and it's stayed with me ever since. Now that I've read the entire collection, I only hope I can make room to keep every one of her poems in my heart and mind tomorrow and beyond.

— **NICOLE ROSS**, author

NO GLASS ALLOWED
Poetry by Tammy Foster Brewer

$12 | 56 pages | 6" x 9" | softcover | ISBN: 978-0615870007

Brewer's collection is filled with uncanny details that readers will wear like the accessories of womanhood. Fishing the Chattahoochee, sideways trees, pollen on a car, white dresses and breast milk, and so much more -- all parts of a deeply intellectual pondering of what is often painful and human regarding the other halves of mothers and daughters, husbands and wives, lovers and lost lovers, children and parents.

— **NICHOLAS BELARDES**
author of *Songs of the Glue Machines*

Tammy deftly juxtaposes distinct imagery with stories that seem to collide in her brilliant poetic mind. Stories of transmissions and trees and the words we utter, or don't. Of floods and forgiveness, conversations and car lanes, bread and beginnings, awe and expectations, desire and leaps of faith that leave one breathless, and renewed.

"When I say I am a poet / I mean my house has many windows" has to be one of the best descriptions of what it's like to be a contemporary female poet who not only holds down a day job and raises a family, but whose mind and heart regularly file away fleeting images and ideas that might later be woven into something permanent, and perhaps even beautiful. This ability is not easily acquired. It takes effort, and time, and the type of determination only some writers, like Tammy, possess and are willing to actively exercise.

— **KAREN DEGROOT CARTER**
author of *One Sister's Song*

DO YOU WRITE POETRY?
Submit it to our biweekly online magazine!

We publish poems every Tuesday & Thursday on website.

Come see what all the fuss is about!

We like Poems that sneak up on you. Poems that make out with you. Poems that bloody your mouth just to kiss it clean. Poems that bite your cheek so you spend all day tonguing the wound. Poems that vandalize your heart. Poems that act like a tin can phone connecting you to your childhood. Fire Alarm Poems. Glitterbomb Poems. Jailbreak Poems. Poems that could marry the land or the sea; that are both the hero & the villain. Poems that are the matches when there is a city-wide power outage. Poems that throw you overboard just dive in & save your ass. Poems that push you down on the stoop in front of history's door screaming at you to knock. Poems that are soft enough to fall asleep on. Poems that will still be clinging to the walls inside of your bones on your 90th birthday. We like poems. Submit yours.

WORDSDANCE.COM